THE SPIRIT AT THE
END OF HISTORY

ISBN: 978-1-7358111-7-8

Mystery School Press
P.O. Box 63767
Philadelphia, PA 19147
mysteryschoolpress.com

Cover and Interior design by Sophie Peirce.

Printed in the United States of America.

THE SPIRIT AT THE END OF HISTORY

A Commentary on Sri Aurobindo's
The Human Cycle

RAVI JOSEPH

MYSTERY SCHOOL PRESS
Philadelphia, Pennsylvania

Over the past four centuries, humanity has progressed towards greater mastery of the physical world through science and technology, while human society has had to undergo a process of continuous adaptation to this advance. This extraordinary knowledge of and mastery over physical nature allows us to synthesize artificial materials, launch satellites which coordinate GPS systems, and transport goods over long distances through logistics networks that are mediated by information technology. These abilities are far beyond those possessed by any human society before us and the continued advance is anticipated to be indefinite. In the language of control theory, a branch of engineering which aims to guide artifacts through complex dynamical systems, we have developed extraordinary "control" capabilities over material forces. In the physical world, our ability to control larger and more complex systems is ever increasing and we often run into the limits of economic and human resources before we hit the limits of engineering.

Despite our ability to control physical systems, our ability to steer the direction of human society is considerably less developed. In the unprecedented affluence of the late 20th and early 21st centuries, one question echoes resoundingly for all thinking people: if our mastery over physical systems and wealth-generating processes is so great, why have we not been able to apply the same ingenuity to the social realm to reach utopia by now? We have the resources needed to feed all humans but there are still people who go hungry. If we are so intelligent, surely we can figure out a way so that we won't have to fight destructive wars any longer. Instead, we still find our societies subject to problems that seem much more primitive than our technologies would seem to indicate.

Though we have progressed to knowledge and technological ability in the realm of physical nature, we are still far away from any comparable knowledge in the realm of human nature. This is not for a lack of trying. A school of thought known as *scientific materialism* proposes that all phenomena in the universe, including the realms of biology and psychology, can be explained in terms of physical laws. Following this philosophy, research projects are under way to raise our knowledge of the human realm to the same level as our knowledge of the physical realm. The biological sciences aim to show that all biological phenomena of growth, reproduction, respiration, metabolism, and so on, and even the genesis of life are a product of the same laws that govern physics and chemistry. Under the influence of this paradigm the sciences of psychiatry, psychology, and cognitive science aim to show that individual human behavior is under the influence of the laws of biology, which can be reduced to the laws of chemistry or physics. And at the level of collective human behavior, the social sciences like sociology and social psychology aim to show that the behavior of human collectives can be reduced to materialist psychology, materialist biology, and materialist physics. But in practice, none of these sciences can directly show how human behavior can be derived from the same laws that govern gravity and electromagnetic fields. These fields have not furnished absolutely foolproof guides to human behavior; they still find themselves surprised: social and political phenomena throughout the 2010's and beyond have been continuously surprising for most observers.

Though the scientific materialist hypothesis seems convincing in the light of the successes of the physical sciences, it has not yet been proven outside the physical realm. The main approach to studying the non-physical human condition remains through the humanities and human sciences. In this context, the question of control over human nature, society, and history can be seen as the applied version of a classic question that has long been asked by these fields: the question of the meaning and direction of history. The question of history in Western philosophy goes back at least as far as the Greeks who developed techniques of narrative history that we still employ today. In the narrative approach, we try to gain an understanding and appreciation of the factors that influenced a given historical event through narrative, in the same way that in a novel or drama we gain an aestheticized understanding of the forces that influence a situational development in a group of characters. For example, a common reading of the fall of the Roman Empire blamed the fall of the empire on a loss of virtue in its people.

Once we see that there are certain forces at work in a given historical development, we are led to wonder if it is possible to apprehend a general set of laws that underlie any sort of historical development at all—perhaps even a master law or direction to history. An understanding of such laws would allow us to elevate the knowledge of human sciences, in particular history, to the same level of knowledge as the natural sciences, like physics. But this concern goes back farther than modern natural science to the early Christians, who combined the knowledge of Greek historical techniques with the idea of a divine meaning to historical unfolding from the Jewish tradition to create the unique vision of history ending in universal salvation brought about by Jesus Christ. By the early modern period, however, it seemed like it was not religious salvation but rather scientific and technological progress that was the key force driving history. These ideas eventually influenced the German idealist historians to work out a secularized "universal history" which aimed to find the meaning of all previous history in terms of a future endpoint that could be known with the right insight.

This brings us to a theory of history, both infamous and inescapable, that has influenced contemporary discourse in the West, Francis Fukuyama's theory of the "end of history." Fukuyama synthesized several threads of history and philosophy to argue that the main mechanisms or forces driving history are first, economic development driven by scientific progress, which leads to educated and prosperous populations and second, an aspect of human nature discussed in the work of philosopher G.W.F. Hegel called the "struggle for recognition," which is the human desire to be seen by the rest of society as having value. Fukuyama argued that the interplay of these two forces in history led the most advanced countries to an "end of history" condition consisting of the liberal democratic state with free-market economic policies, with the less developed countries inevitably following them in time.

Fukuyama's text, published in 1992, contrasted with a background of 20th century thinking that was skeptical of the sort of grand narrativizing by earlier philosophers like Hegel. However, it became highly influential because it seemed to provide a coherent account of the success of liberal democracy through the 1990's and 2000's, and remains credible on a high level even today. The events of the 2010s such as a worldwide wave of right-wing populism and the rise of China's illiberal regime would seem to cast doubt on his thesis; though in fact the latter part of his book addressed the possibilities of nationalism and right-wing populism having a resurgence. The main questions for the validity of his argument at this point seem to be first, whether China represents a viable alternate option for societal development and stability and second, whether democracies can handle the impact of social media technology on rational discourse in the public sphere.

My concern here, however, is not to establish whether Fukuyama is right or wrong, but rather to contextualize the work of another thinker who came to different conclusions about a similar set of questions. In his book *The Human Cycle*, Sri Aurobindo set out his own vision of social and historical evolution, though he ultimately found spiritual rather than primarily material factors at work. Sri Aurobindo is best known for his philosophy of spiritual transformation, set out in works like *The Life Divine*, *The Synthesis of Yoga*, and his voluminous correspondence, and enacted in the living experiment of the Sri Aurobindo Ashram in India. But he had long been a student of the European political tradition, studying at Cambridge and absorbing the political and cultural history of Europe; he was also an active participant in the struggle for Indian independence, though he refrained from political participation after his spiritual turn. *The Human Cycle* is in fact an extension of his spiritual writing and not an exception to it. This is because Sri Aurobindo's spiritual philosophy is a life affirming vision which holds that the activities of earthly life, including the social and, eventually, political life must be recast in a spiritual vision.

In *The Human Cycle*, Sri Aurobindo considers the development of societies with a view towards understanding the future, particularly in light of social and political issues from the time of its writing in the early 20th century. Like some of the earlier historians and philosophers, Sri Aurobindo saw outer factors like economics and outward human psychology as critical factors influencing the development of civilization. However, he did not view the "end of history" in the same way Fukuyama did. Instead, he believed human society could only come to full flower in a spiritual age—one in which all humans have the ability to develop their outer being in line with the truth of their soul or inner spirit. And this is because the rational mind proves ultimately unable to deal with the complexities and movements of life. This view is not equivalent to an endorsement of irrationalism as, in his view, a rational age is an essential precursor to this age of the spirit, since a society in which the mind is not developed fully throughout its population can only lapse again and again into ignorance. But even in a society where the mind is fully developed and devoted to the problems of complex social organization, the great liberal ideals of liberty, equality, and fraternity prove impossible to balance in a rational system, whether by political genius or technocratic machinery or any other faculty of the mind. In Sri Aurobindo's view, only through the unveiling of the inner spirit can fullness and harmony be reached on Earth.

The Meaning of History for Sri Aurobindo

The transition to the spiritual age is the one that we as a civilization are still navigating, and it comes at a quite advanced stage of societal development. In the terms Sri Aurobindo uses in the text, it is the transition from the individualist, or rational, stage to the subjective, or spiritual stage. ("Individualism" and "rationalism" are not quite the same but are equivalent stages in our society for historically contingent reasons, and the terms are used interchangeably where appropriate; similarly, a "subjective" age may or may not be "spiritual", but since Sri Aurobindo forecasted a subjective age that was spiritual as well, the terms are sometimes used interchangeably.) Several earlier stages of societal evolution come before it; the cycle in full is made of the symbolic, typal, conventional, individualist, and finally subjective age. Sri Aurobindo borrowed the names of these stages from a historian named Karl Lamprecht whose work he encountered. However, Sri Aurobindo did not choose to borrow his entire analytic framework, rather choosing to borrow only the names of the stages because of their suggestive significance (*HC* 6).

In Sri Aurobindo's theory, any society progresses through these five stages, though he most frequently discusses Western and Indian examples. In theory, different societies could be at different stages of the cycle. Indeed, societies evolved separately for much of human history because they were physically separated and were not connected by the instantaneous communication flows which connect the planet now. However, at this point in history all societies and civilizations are knit into one supra-civilization. Because of the dominance of physical science, every society needs to industrialize and deploy the latest technologies to remain economically and militarily competitive, meaning that every functioning nation-state has at least a segment of its society in the individualistic rational age. There are still major divides in societal and cultural development between countries—the question of whether China and the West can be assessed along the same scale or if they progress in incommensurable ways is a still-open question. However, for the most part, human civilization on the whole is currently still undergoing the transition from the individualist to the subjective stage.

And here we get to the main difference between Sri Aurobindo's theory and other mainstream forms of historical theory. Sri Aurobindo believed that the main mechanism driving history is spiritual evolution, rather than a materialist factor like technology or economics, or even human psychology in its outward levels. This spirit is the Divine essence in the human individual, and it is not the same as the individual's outer psychology. Fukuyama also notes that a materialist explanation invoking science, technology, and economics is not enough to explain all the developments of history, as otherwise we might see authoritarian capitalism accepted everywhere as the governmental model instead of a persistently stable form of liberal democracy seen in major countries in the West, and major eastern powers like Japan and India (Fukuyama 134). But he completes his explanation without reference to the Divine by incorporating the idea of the "struggle for recognition," an aspect of human nature discussed by Hegel and elaborated by Alexandre Kojève. Fukuyama finds this aspect of human nature discussed under different names throughout the development of Western political theory, such as in the Greek concept of thymos and the aristocratic idea of virtue stemming from military victory which dominated culture and politics before the ascendance of liberalism. In Fukuyama's framework, this struggle for recognition causes disenfranchised segments of society to demand political equality, which leads to a convergence in governments towards liberal democracy.

For Sri Aurobindo, this aspect of human nature is indeed important, and perhaps he would even agree with Fukuyama that it is less recognized in discourse than it should be. Indeed, a difference between Fukuyama and Sri Aurobindo is that Sri Aurobindo recognizes a greater variety of psychological factors at work, identifying such disparate qualities as courage, honor, pride, aggression, and aristocratic virtue as many different elements in a complex plane of existence that he terms the "vital." But even viewing human psychology as being made up of the mind, desire, plus the struggle for recognition as in Fukuyama's psychology does not penetrate far enough to the root of the problem. What is missing can only be found by peering into the *soul* of the human individual. This is the part of human psychology that knows light, beauty, love, freedom—in short, all the Divine principles. These principles find political expression in the great liberal trinity of values, liberty (freedom), equality, and fraternity (brotherhood), which Sri Aurobindo viewed as "three godheads of the soul" (Sri Aurobindo, *Ideal of Human Unity* 569). The development of history for Sri Aurobindo is not simply the story of the development of economics, mind, culture, and technology, or even the vital emotions and qualities like honor, prestige, and recognition—though all of these have their place. The development of human history is that of the soul working through progressive forms in its evolution towards the Divine.

The Early Ages of The Cycle

The first few ages of the human cycle—the symbolic, typal, and conventional ages—are discussed in quick succession in chapter 1 as the main problematic of the text is about the nature of the rationalistic individualist age and the transition to the subjective age. The first age in the cycle is the symbolic age. In the symbolic age, all movements of life are viewed as symbols of a greater reality without the need for rational explanation that is characteristic of our modern age. Because this is so different from the basis of modern life, the spirit of this age can be hard for our modern mindset to enter into. Sri Aurobindo discusses in particular the Vedic age in India, where life was governed by the symbol of "sacrifice." This is an unfamiliar idea for modern people. We may be prepared to sacrifice specific things for specific ends, like sacrificing free time to earn money for a family, but the vision of the entirety of life as a sacrifice to the Gods is a foreign idea. After the symbolic age, the patterns of society settle in and each station of society is seen to have a particular role, function, or in the Indian philosophical terminology, its own *dharma*. An example of this stage would be medieval Europe, where there were codes of chivalry for knights and an ethic of labor for peasants that were upheld by the idea of maintaining the honor of the social class. From the typal stage, society hardens further into the conventional stage, where there is no reason or value given at all as a justification for societal arrangements, only the argument that the arrangements come from age-old tradition; the arrangements are of course enforced by a rigid church or central government.

This evolution from the symbolic into the typal and conventional stages can be seen as a process where a living symbolic mentality arises, and then progressively gets further and further solidified in the outer form of matter. "For always the form prevails and the spirit recedes and diminishes. It attempts indeed to return, to revive the form, to modify it, anyhow to survive and even to make the form survive; but the time-tendency is too strong" (*HC* 13). The creative process of the spirit creates forms with more and more detail, and the nature of matter is to preserve these forms. An intuitive, symbolic mentality is cast up, its possibilities are worked out and types evolve and become more definite, and then finally a conventional stage sets in where the forms are hardened almost to the point of immobility. But this very process of the spirit developing its own possibilities to the fullest extent and realizing its forms outwardly results in a situation where the spirit has less and less freedom and space to act according to its own inmost ideas and tendencies.

This leads to the individualist age of humanity. In chapter 2, the transition from the conventional to the individualist age is elaborated at more length than the previous transitions, because our current society still reverberates with its great moments, like the challenges of Luther and Galileo which have a nearly mythical significance. During the conventional stage, the individual is completely bound within the structures and conventions of the established institutions. They are not free to question the positions or the actions they are compelled to take: only the positions given by the authorities are acceptable, and there is no possibility of free thought or action. Yet the established positions are not felt to have any true inner reason or nourishment for the spirit. Whereas in the original symbolic age, actions were invested with meaning and purpose that did not need any explanation, as they were naturally fulfilling for the soul, and then later in the typal age when they were solidified, at least the principle of upholding the honor of dharma provided spiritual substance, in the conventional age the outer form has hardened too much and the principle of matter has led to too much inertia, so that the spirit can no longer feel or express its true nature. Because the inner spirit is the real driver for the evolutionary process, the spirit must try to find its way to a new possibility of fulfillment, which it does by working through the individual to rediscover a true principle of life. "And it is necessarily individualistic, because all the old general standards have become bankrupt and can no longer give any inner help; it is therefore the individual who has to become a discoverer, a pioneer, and to search out by his individual reason, intuition, idealism, desire, claim upon life or whatever other light he finds in himself the true law of the world and of his own being" (*HC* 15).

The paradigmatic example discussed is the Reformation, the great assertion of the individual search for truth in Western culture. In this movement, the individual asserted the ability to relate to God without dependence on the Catholic Church's claim to be the unique intermediary between humanity and God. But while the Reformation was the first awakening of reason, ultimately even its conclusions could be questioned, and Sri Aurobindo notes that "eventually, the evolution of Europe was determined less by the Reformation than by the Renascence [Renaissance]" (*HC* 19) in that the Renaissance found in ancient Greece and Rome positive examples for free philosophical questioning and mastery of life.

The problem that such an individualist age will encounter is how to organize society when all individuals are free to pursue the truth they see fit without the rigid societal arrangements provided by the conventional stage. Sri Aurobindo notes that European society found a suitable principle with the development of science (*HC* 20). Science provided a truth which was verifiable and accessible to all of humanity, without the need for any priesthood; it found its truths directly from Nature which was accessible to direct sensory observation and did not rely on esoteric spiritual knowledge or unquestionable acts of interpretation as previous orders used to justify their system. And this is the basis of shared knowledge our society still has. While our society still allows people to have freedom of belief and religion in their private lives, in the issues that matter most for the fundamentals of life—such as economic and military organization—the rule of science is still unchallenged, and science sets the standard for truth in the public square (even if political debates do not always rise to that standard).

But this principle of shared knowledge of materialist science leads to tensions that we are still grappling with over 100 years after the writing of the text. Materialist science eventually must discover the truth of humankind as a biological species whose aim is to perpetuate itself, with no higher material justification, and that discovery could lead to a justification for reinstitution of forms of social organization which end up being similar to the conventional age again. In a passage which strongly resonates with current debates on social science, technology and administrative organization, Sri Aurobindo writes "In place of the religio-ethical sanction there will be a scientific and rational or naturalistic motive and rule; instead of the Brahmin Shastrakara the scientific, administrative and economic expert" going on to note that education, career choice, and even marriage could be dictated by the science-informed State (*HC* 21). Indeed, the field of "social science" claims the right to investigate and guide policy on all of these matters, though there are different interpretations as to how far we are on the road to such a totalizing condition as described by the quote.

This would seem to raise the possibility of lapsing into a conventional age once again, with the truths discovered by social science serving as the new inflexible rules of society. But according to Sri Aurobindo, there are other dynamics in play that could avert this possibility (*HC* 22). There is first of all the discovery of a new inner world in psychology, art, and philosophy that opens the doorway to a new "subjective age" that would succeed the individualist age. The second factor was the awakening of Asia to its full power. At the time the book was written in the early 20th Century, many Asian countries were still colonies of the West, and were not yet industrialized; this changed in the 20th century with the liberation of European colonies in Asia, and the process of industrialization which is still ongoing. We continue to witness how the political and economic rise of these nations is changing the geopolitical equations that the world was previously based on. But in this passage Sri Aurobindo suggested that the ideas coming from Asia—especially the spiritual thought of India, as he emphasized in other works—would have a large effect on the world, as opposed to its economic rise alone. One hundred years later, we can see that this is true, with the concepts of meditation and hatha yoga from the Indian subcontinent spreading worldwide, and more knowledge sure to come. Thirdly, there is the increasing acceptance of the importance of the individual soul as opposed to the previous consensus which regarded the individual as only a cog in society's machine. In summary, the influences from the inner world in art and psychology, the rise of spiritual ideas from Asia, and the increasing acceptance of the importance of the individual could together provide a countervailing force against a rigid scientific materialism and could perhaps help to open the subjective age. But just what is this subjective age that Sri Aurobindo believed would come next? He explores this in chapters 3-7.

The Fulfillment of Humanity in the Subjective Age

To understand the meaning of the subjective age, we must go back to understand the link between the preceding individualist age and objectivity. Earlier, we noted that the individualist age could as well be called the rationalistic age. In the general schema of the procession of ages, the individualist age will come after the conventional age because it is only the individual who can break through the stifling demands of the conventional order of society to find a new law of action and being. In our particular Western society, the new law of social being ended up being the ideal of rationality, inherited from Greece, and the practical, utilitarian spirit inherited from Rome, both of which were passed on through the Renaissance. This law of social being informs the demand we make on each individual person to live life and participate in society according to reason, and also informs the way we organize society, submitting all laws and institutions to the criterion of rationality. This is in contrast to previous ages of society where individual actions, interpersonal relations, and societal organization were justified only by custom or faith. Thus, the individualist age is also a rational age. But in addition to being rational, this individualist age is also objective—meaning that it regards life and the world as an object that can be manipulated. The scientific mind analyzes the physical world to find out its laws, determining the nature and structure of physical phenomena like light, heat, and gravity, and manipulates these laws to secure technological power for humanity, allowing it to build bridges, construct transport systems, and create new synthetic materials. But this mind does not only regard the physical world as an object: it subjects everything else to this same method of scrutiny as well. Plant, animal, and human life are interrogated as complex chemical mechanisms, and scientists seek to understand their input and output pathways. Even the social world is regarded with rational scrutiny, as scientists seek to formulate statistical laws that can predict human behavior under various conditions, in order to secure societally recognized goods like order and safety.

For Sri Aurobindo, this process can go only so far before running past its own limits. "But after a time it must become apparent that the knowledge of the physical world is not the whole of knowledge; it must appear that man is a mental as well as a physical and vital being and even much more essentially mental than physical or vital... in his study of himself and the world he cannot but come face to face with the soul in himself and the soul in the world and find it to be an entity so profound, so complex, so full of hidden secrets and powers that his intellectual reason betrays itself as an insufficient light and a fumbling seeker..." (*HC* 28-29). In other words, the very process of exploring the limits of the rationalistic paradigm must eventually lead past the rationalistic paradigm and into something else, because the human spirit contains complexities that cannot be known by the rationalistic paradigm.

Within the rationalistic paradigm itself, of course, it would not be admitted that humanity has any aspect that cannot be known from an objective, rationalistic perspective; because Sri Aurobindo believes that there is an aspect of humanity that cannot be known by such an objective, rationalistic perspective, he is already working from a framework outside that perspective. In fact, we know that he was engaged with the practice of Yoga, a form of spiritual discipline, and had in his own view obtained access to forms of spiritual and intuitive knowledge that could not be gained from the rational intellect alone. Therefore, to the pure rationalist, the idea that the rational search must lead beyond rationality may not seem convincing; the pure rationalist would believe that the program of seeking all knowledge of the psychological and social being and how to organize it proceeding on scientific lines alone is still valid, and that the idea of any further subjective age is not possible. Therefore the reader who is poised to fully absorb the message of the text is someone who is at least open to the idea that there could be some other possibility of knowledge besides objective, rationalistic knowledge, even though they do not have to have the same level or form of the specifically spiritual knowledge that Sri Aurobindo achieved.

And what are these secret aspects of the psychological nature that cannot be gained from a rationalistic, objective model alone? This is the realm of the subjective, and it includes all the aspects of experience that are left out of the objective view. Only those who have experienced it can speak of it truly—and those who would adhere to scientific materialism without the experience of the inner world would not admit its existence. But it can be glimpsed in all those domains outside the purely scientific materialist worldview. Sri Aurobindo reviews several characteristic examples of a subjective view in chapter 3, "The Coming of the Subjective Age." First, there is the inner and subjective spiritual worldview from India that he believed would be increasingly influential on the West. Another example was the philosophy of Friedrich Nietzsche, who recovered the life-principle in philosophy. Another important source of examples was in the latest developments of literature of the period, such as Russian literature, which viewed humanity with special psychological insight. Though he does not discuss this in the chapter, we can most likely add the Romantic movement of the 18th-19th centuries as another example; Sri Aurobindo was profoundly influenced by the work of English Romantic poets like John Keats and Percy Shelley.

Another example he gives to characterize the subjective view is education. The idea of mass education grew prominent in the industrial age, and while it served a great positive effect in bringing education to many groups of people who lacked access to it before, it had the drawback of being overly rigid and shaping children's minds in a cookie-cutter form. Some critics of this form of education liken it to being a factory for children's minds. A subjective view on education would rather proceed from "the realisation that each human being is a self-developing soul and that the business of both parent and teacher is to enable and to help the child to educate himself, to develop his own intellectual, moral, aesthetic and practical capacities and to grow freely as an organic being, not to be kneaded and pressured into form like an inert plastic material" (*HC* 33). The debate over how and what children should be taught still continues. But while the pragmatic questions such as how children are to be given all the necessary material needed for success in the world, how they can be socialized properly with other children, and how this can be done within societal institutions in a cost-effective way are not yet resolved, the general principle that each child is a unique soul whose nature deserves to be respected is increasingly accepted as a foundational axiom of education.

To these trends that were visible to Sri Aurobindo's view in the early 20th century, we can add at least two more. First, the domain of work. Just as education has changed in its attitude from trying to mold a child's mind into predefined inflexible patterns to an attempt at bringing out a child's inner qualities and talents, so has the domain of work seen a change from the idea that people need to be prepared to perform whatever dull or backbreaking labor is assigned to them, to the idea that individuals have unique skills and talents and should have the opportunity to do work that they are passionate about. In the older way of thinking, labeled "Theory X" by management theorist Douglas McGregor, the employee is viewed as being fundamentally untrustworthy and needs to be compelled to do the unpleasant task of work, while in the newer model, labeled "Theory Y" by McGregor, the employee is trusted and given autonomy to do the tasks that they find most interesting and fulfilling to advance the goals of the organization (Bolman and Deal 105). Just as the subjective ideal of education is imperfectly realized, the subjective theory of work is imperfectly realized even in the most progressive workplaces. However, like with education, the theory is increasingly admitted, at least as an ideal to reach; and since it is most zealously pursued by the most innovative individuals in the leading societies, employers are compelled to accommodate it to at least some degree.

The second domain of increasing subjectivity is the realm of psychotherapy. Sri Aurobindo was familiar with the initial developments in psychoanalysis from the work of Sigmund Freud, who was the most influential figure in bringing the psychoanalytic worldview into the mainstream. He viewed Freud's work with suspicion, believing that it was a questionable way to access inner realities and that it put too much emphasis on the lower drives of human nature like power and sexuality at the expense of higher mental ideals, and explicitly neglected the spiritual dimension entirely (Sri Aurobindo, *Letters of Yoga vol. 4* 612). However, a century later we can see a great variety of approaches to therapy, some which are still psychoanalytic, but some which are more scientific, others more humanistic, and some even incorporating elements from spiritual philosophies. While many are influenced to some extent by Freud, and all are indebted to his work in bringing the therapeutic method to widespread recognition, most do not adhere strictly to his theories that reduce human motivation to base drives. Most of the work people do in contemporary psychotherapy is examining their feelings, experiences, and motivations to get to a state of increased well being—in other words, looking into their subjective selves within the context of a society that is still largely identified with the objective.

In chapters 4 and 5, Sri Aurobindo explores the phenomenon of nationhood from the perspective of the subjective age. Just as there is a subjective principle that applies to the individual in domains like education, work, and therapy, so is there a subjective principle that applies to entire groups of people; a community of people has its own values and tendencies, and even its own *dharma*, or law of being, just as an individual does. The danger, as was already recognized by the time of the text's writing, is that these national attachments can lead to clashes, conquests, and other forms of violence and domination. However, Sri Aurobindo noted that this was due to an egoic nationalism; just as individuals can have unique and differentiated personalities and ways of being but get along harmoniously after transcending the ego principle, so could nations maintain their own separate tendencies but live harmoniously alongside each other by getting past the egoic dimensions of nationalism.

Thus it is in the subjective age that the deepest potentials of humanity in society are fulfilled; and that is why the human spirit works teleologically to lead history to this end. As Sri Aurobindo explains in chapter 7, "The Ideal Law of Social Development", it is in the subjective age that the individual human and the broader community each have their best chance to work out their own unique tendencies of being. Further, from a metaphysical perspective it is the expression of this tendency of being that is the very purpose of the manifestation in the universe, so it makes sense that this would be the ideal law of society. The role of the individual is to discover their own way of being, use that to contribute to the life of the community and through that to the entirety of humankind. The role of the community or nation is to allow the individual a chance to develop his or her own talents and way of being and harmonize with it, but also to have a fulfilling and peaceful interchange with other communities free from domination and conflict. "Thus the community stands as a mid-term and intermediary value between the individual and humanity and it exists not merely for itself, but for the one and the other and to help them to fulfil each other" (*HC* 69). And, once again, ideally, this would take place in a condition of freedom. Sri Aurobindo continually insists that it is not through the imposition of any outward system, be it an educational system, governmental system, or system of ethics or religion that the individual can reach this perfection. "No State or legislator or reformer can cut him rigorously into a perfect pattern; no Church or priest can give him a mechanical salvation; no order, no class life or ideal, no nation, no civilisation or creed or ethical, social or religious Shastra can be allowed to say to him permanently, 'In this way of mine and thus far shalt thou act and grow and in no other way and no farther shall thy growth be permitted'" (*HC* 67).

This is one of the places where we can see the sharpest contrast between Sri Aurobindo's vision and other teleological sociopolitical visions such as those of Fukuyama and his predecessor Hegel: Sri Aurobindo's vision does not predict that the state of the freedom of humanity will end in any specific system or form of government; no system or form will be adequate, though of course at any given time one form or another will be in place. But in particular, this form will not necessarily be the ideal of the rational, universal liberal state envisioned by Hegel where each human stands in direct relation to the universal, nor will it necessarily be the worldwide spread of the post-Cold War neoliberal system envisioned by Fukuyama. This is for at least two reasons. First, the universal visions miss the potential for each nation or community to find a unique way of being—including a unique way of life and possibly a unique form of government—though they will need to learn to cooperate with each other without strife and also harmonize with the freedom of the individual. Second, both the rationalized universal liberal state envisioned by Hegel and the neoliberal elaboration of Fukuyama still fall within the individualistic, rationalistic paradigm, whereas the subjective age comes after the individualistic, rationalistic paradigm has exhausted itself. But this does not mean discarding the gains that these rationalistic forms of societal organization have brought about: as we will see, the subjective principle requires going farther than rationalism, rather than throwing it away. In the next section, Sri Aurobindo surveys the tendencies and tensions, including those of the mind and reason, that lead to the possibility of the Subjective Age.

Civilization and Mental Culture

The next section, comprising chapters 8-12, concerns itself with the question of civilization and the mind. "Civilization" can be an opaque term for us now because it is a total surround: there is nowhere you can go that is outside the reach of modern civilization and its technology. The existence of modern electronic communication technology means that we can travel to nearly any point on the planet and receive the latest political, financial, and cultural news broadcast. Much of our day-to-day work, social communication, and culture is mediated by information flowing through our devices, and if we are caught up in the flow of text and images, the massive technological edifice that allows all this to happen can fade into the background. But in truth, this condition was brought about over centuries of civilization's technological and economic development.

If the notion of "civilization" is opaque, the idea of "barbarism" is even moreso, as this is another concept that is rarely invoked in our discourse; like the word "savage," it is seen to be almost offensive to the egalitarian sensibility of our times which views all cultures as having some value. As a result, we do not perceive the existence of "barbarians" anywhere. To understand what Sri Aurobindo means by the contrast he invokes in the title to chapter 8, "Civilisation and Barbarism," then, we must remember that he was a keen student of classical culture, and his usage of the concept of barbarism is no doubt influenced by his study of classical civilizations in addition to the ideas that were present at the time of writing. The word "barbarian" derives from Greek, and originally referred to any peoples that did not follow Greek cultural practices. But the classic case study in civilization vs. barbarism for the Western mind is the story of the fall of Rome. Rome was the largest empire ever known to Western history before the modern period and provided centuries of civilized living in conditions of peace known as the *Pax Romana*. Within the boundaries of the Roman empire, people enjoyed a right to citizenship, trade, military glory, and sophisticated political structures. But on the outskirts of Rome, there were "barbarian" tribes who did not possess the same level of social and political structure but would invade the outskirts. The main body of the Empire was able to defend itself against these barbarians until a point when it failed, succumbing to barbarian invasion and dissolution of the empire. A common interpretation holds that this long period of civilization ultimately failed to survive because it was surrounded by tribes that were full of energy and jealous for the fruits of civilization without wanting to submit to civilized standards of cultural development.

The characteristic nature of the barbarian is the emphasis on brute physical strength, declining to undertake or even despising the possibility of mental knowledge and ethical development. The idea that brute physical strength could be taken seriously as a goal and measure of humanity is so far from our view that it does not even occur to us to identify it as barbarism as such. Sri Aurobindo notes that the development of modern science makes it highly unlikely that civilization will face the same threat from true barbarism again: science gives us forms of defense and economic organization that make it impossible for it to be defeated by brute physical strength "unless it ceases to be uncivilised and acquires the knowledge which Science alone can give" (*HC* 77). However, this condition leads to still other problems that we must be on the lookout for, such as the problem of securing humanity against the possibility of war between civilized societies with modern weaponry.

A more profound problem with the scientific age of civilization is what Sri Aurobindo calls the "economic barbarian," who makes "the satisfaction of wants and desires and the accumulation of possessions his standard and aim. His ideal man is not the cultured or noble or thoughtful or moral or religious, but the successful man" (*HC* 79). This echoes critiques leveled against the economically successful but culturally barren bourgeois for hundreds of years. Someone under the influence of this type of economic barbarism will care nothing for other people or for higher, nobler values, but only for economic success and the outward trappings that it brings. "The accumulation of wealth and more wealth, the adding of possessions to possessions, opulence, show, pleasure, a cumbrous inartistic luxury, a plethora of conveniences, life devoid of beauty and nobility, religion vulgarised or coldly formalised, politics and government turned into a trade and profession, enjoyment itself made a business, this is commercialism" (*HC* 80). Still, the step to science, technology and industry is not to be despised. "...she [Nature] evidently means him not only to control, create and constantly re-create in new and better forms himself, his own inner existence, his mentality, but also to control and re-create correspondingly his environment. He has to turn Mind not only on itself, but on Life and Matter and the material existence...." (*HC* 83).

There is a further step from the state of organized and governed society, to the level of culture, in which the true higher values come out. Sri Aurobindo follows the Greeks in classing these major values as the intellectual, the ethical, and the aesthetic—in other words, the True, the Good, and the Beautiful, a message taken from antiquity and immortalized for the modern mind in poet John Keats' "Ode on a Grecian Urn." These are characteristic values of the developing human mind. To be concerned with these values at all is to be at a civilized or at least a semi-civilized state, as opposed to still being at the barbaric level of the reign of force. But even within the realm of civilization, there is still a difficulty in reaching the highest levels of values. One of the great values of modern civilization is its egalitarian nature: we have internalized the idea that all people are worthy of respect, and deserve as much chance to develop themselves through education as they are reasonably able to acquire. However, it can be difficult to extend the highest levels of training in these great values to all citizens across the board.

This is a difficult problem to solve, and to our credit, we attempt the solution, whereas past societies were content to reserve the best educational and developmental opportunities for those from privileged classes. There is an issue that can arise from the attempt, though, which is the phenomenon of "philistinism"— a level of cultivation that is higher than the barbarian, but still short of the highest levels of culture. For the philistine, ethical culture is the popular opinion of the right way to act rather than profound knowledge, beauty is a pleasant but mediocre painted scene instead of something with true formal and emotional richness, and knowledge is keeping up with the latest opinion pieces instead of reflection on the great intellectual work of humanity. In his novel *Howard's End*, E.M. Forster provided an empathetic yet ultimately harsh portrait of Leonard Bast, a young clerk who was caught in this middle ground of being in a philistinic state and drawn towards higher values but lacking the leisure to bring them out in his life; ultimately he was not able to cross the chasm. Sri Aurobindo notes that this democratization of higher values in the present society has had "both good and bad results," but was optimistic about letting this trend take its course to see what positive results it may bring (*HC* 91).

Philistinism is the result of the failure to elevate the entire society to the highest level of the intellectual, ethical, and aesthetic ideals. But a subtler issue is that even the highest levels of these three ideals do not inherently harmonize. In chapter 10, "Aesthetic and Ethical Culture," Sri Aurobindo explores the conflict between the aesthetic and the ethical principles—the ethical and Good on one hand, and Beauty on the other. We see this conflict play out in current society. Today, those who pursue the principle of Beauty most strenuously are the artists—painters, filmmakers, musicians, writers, and so on. Because our society is so dominated by the commercial impulse, most other members of society must spend time in un-aesthetic surroundings of the commercial and industrial world with only a small amount of time, if any, for aesthetic pleasures. It is them, the workers, who are regarded as responsible and upstanding citizens who uphold society and economic production. Artists, in contrast, must generally reject the values of the business world, as they need time to work on their craft; thus they are seen as shiftless or irresponsible in not upholding the responsible values of the business world. Further, they are more permissive in their attitudes towards taboo moral matters such as drugs and sexuality in their search for novel experiences. Poet Samuel Coleridge's opium visions, the association of jazz musicians with drug usage in the early 20th century, the death of any number of rock stars from drug overdoses—all these examples affirm the link between artists and moral license. Of course, the supposedly "responsible" bourgeois often have vices of their own, though they proceed in discreet, private ways, like alcoholism and adultery. But on the whole, the principle of beauty tends to flee from the limits set by the ethical mind to regulate life.

But the examples of the modern world did not capture the essence of the phenomena Sri Aurobindo intended to point out; he cited the middle-class morality of England at the time, which is more or less comparable to our present society, as one example of a certain kind of ethical strain that was not in fact the most characteristic form of the ethical tendency (*HC* 96). Rather, the purest examples of the ethical and aesthetic types for him were found in the ancient world in republican Rome and ancient Athens, respectively. The spirit of these two civilizations may be difficult for the modern mind to enter into, but we may try to understand what it is that he saw in these examples. In Rome he saw "an almost unique experiment in high and strong character-building divorced as far as may be from the sweetness which the sense of beauty and the light which the play of the reason brings into character and uninspired by the religious temperament... the human will oppressing and disciplining the emotional and sensational mind in order to arrive at the self-mastery of a definite ethical type" (*HC* 97). Indeed, it did not even matter that the ethical ideal was not the same as our modern ideal, as the ethical ideal changes from age to age—what was important was the refinement of the character by the will. In contrast, the modern bourgeois civilizations have a much more live-and-let-live attitude, perhaps due to our awareness of the relativity of ethical ideals, but also perhaps because our society is indeed not one of those which pursue the line of severe ethical development with the same strenuousness.

He found the ideal of Beauty, on the other hand, developed most intensely in the first period of ancient Athenian civilization where "the sense of beauty and the need of freedom of life and the enjoyment of life are the determining forces. This Athens thought, but it thought in the terms of art and poetry, in figures of music and drama and architecture and sculpture; it delighted in intellectual discussion, but not so much with any will to arrive at truth as for the pleasure of thinking and the beauty of ideas" (*HC* 99). Just as our society, and most societies, do not exhibit the strenuousness of the pursuit of the ethical ideal evinced by Rome, so do we not pursue beauty with the same intensity as was seen in Athens. But neither the high pursuit of ethics nor the high pursuit of beauty was able to truly master life for society. According to one famous explanation of the fall of Rome, Rome eventually lost its virtue, from perhaps exhaustion or the return of the repressed. Similarly, Sri Aurobindo notes that the worship of beauty led to a condition where Athens "exhausted its vitality within one wonderful century which left it enervated, will-less, unable to succeed in the struggle of life, uncreative" (*HC* 99). We understand this informally at the level of life advice: too much license in pursuit of the beautiful leads to a lack of structure in life, but too much ethical structure without beauty and pleasure leads to a barren and joyless existence.

The search for the faculty that can organize life leads us to the third of the great values, Truth, and the domain of rational intelligence through which it manifests in humanity. In both the Indian and the Western traditions of philosophy the principle of the truth has been identified as the highest power inherent in humanity, with Aristotle defining the human as the rational animal and the Indian tradition identifying the importance of the faculty of the *buddhi*, or intelligent will. Sri Aurobindo is unequivocal about the importance of humanity's capacity for rational intelligence. "Reason using the intelligent will for the ordering of the inner and the outer life is undoubtedly the highest developed faculty of man at his present point of evolution" (*HC* 102). When we compare the rule of reason over life to the rule of war and brute force, to the rule of a cloistered and uninterpretable religion, or to the possibility of rule by closed networks of elites, we would affirm that administering the organization of life by rational rule is certainly the highest and best.

And yet there is the suspicion that reason is somehow not up to the task. The human mind tries to sound the depths of its condition with science and philosophy, and eventually does even reach certain successes, being able to send probes to distant planets or crafts under the sea. But this is still the mastery of the physical world; to deal with life humans have to understand the psychology and behavior of their fellow humans. And they come to the conclusion that, in fact, the rational part of the human mind is not its only part. The most rational psychology still has to come face to face with the fact that all humans contain forces like anger, lust, and desire for possession. The mind has to grapple with the fact that it is not possible to perfectly reconcile competing claims such as historical versus present injustices. And in the 20th century it came face to face with the conclusion that it cannot simply wipe the slate clean and build a new, rational order on top of a blank slate, as both authoritarian left- and right-wing governments discovered, and as political scientist James C. Scott discussed in *Seeing Like a State*.

To govern the world by reason requires dealing with the phenomenon of *life*, and this is not a task that can be done easily. If life cannot be mastered by the mind, perhaps one could make the attempt to cast away the reason entirely and delve headlong into the passions and urges of life. But this is a dead end—if not because of the concern for immorality, as in the case of the artist who pursues beauty at all costs, then because this is simply not an effective way to work in the modern industrialized world; mastery of scientific rationality is an imperative if only from the need to compete militarily and economically. Then perhaps one might think the solution is to make the idea the governor of life at any cost. But this is not easy, as the mind is dominated by the interests of the one who wields it, the success of an idea is always partial, and there are always competing theories. Sri Aurobindo thus comes to the position of the skeptic of the right of the mind to rule absolutely: "This is the cause why all human systems have failed in the end; for they have never been anything but a partial and confused application of reason to life. Moreover, even where they have been most clear and rational, these systems have pretended that their ideas were the whole truth of life and tried so to apply them" (*HC* 108).

Mind always applies itself to life in a partial way because that is the essential nature of mind and the essential nature of life. This is not to say that the effort should not be attempted, as all potentials need to be worked out, and we are not able to discard the effort at mental and rational organization yet. However, we must recognize the more profound underlying metaphysical truth, that the world and life are manifestations of an Infinite existence beyond the mind and are not fully understood or represented by it. "Behind everything in life there is an Absolute, which that thing is seeking after in its own way; everything finite is striving to express an infinite which it feels to be its real truth. Moreover, it is not only each class, each type, each tendency in Nature that is thus impelled to strive after its own secret truth in its own way, but each individual brings in his own variations. Thus there is not only an Absolute, an Infinite in itself which governs its own expression in many forms and tendencies, but there is also a principle of infinite potentiality and variation quite baffling to the reasoning intelligence; for the reason deals successfully only with the settled and the finite" (*HC* 112). In this greater context, mind is not seen as an absolute and sovereign power, but rather as an intermediate power that regulates and balances the work of a force that comes from beyond the mind. Neither is this force the mere life-urge; the life-urge is insufficient to administer a modern government or industrial organization, and the mind is needed, and yet it is still insufficient to fully understand the true will that is operating behind. The process of mental knowledge is "governed by a number of conflicting ideas and ideals around which these experiments group themselves: each of them is gradually pushed as far as possible in its purity and again mixed and combined as much as possible with others so that there may be a more complex form and an enriched action. Each type has to be broken in turn to yield place to new types and each combination has to give way to the possibility of a new combination" (*HC* 118).

Since the complex aspects of human psychology seem to conflict with each other, there was the supposition that reason could be the faculty that organizes the life of civilization and allows it to proceed. But when we look at the nature of the mind, we see that the principles, reasonings, and ideals of the mind can never grasp the absolute—the nature of the progressive developing mind is rather a series of experiments, developments, and partial syntheses that never grasp the whole of the Absolute in its entirety. If it is not reason that is most directly attuned with the nature of the Absolute Reality, then perhaps a more direct attunement to this Absolute would be a better guide to life. Is it possible that religion, the domain which has inquired most directly into the nature of this Absolute, is a more proper and effective governor of the life of humanity? In chapters 13-17, Sri Aurobindo considers the possibilities and limitations of governing life by the religious principle.

The Possibilities and Limitations of Religion as a Guide to Life

The attempt to govern life by the rational mind, while appropriate to humanity's current stage of development, cannot ultimately succeed. The attempt of mentally imposed ideals and standards to bring about true truth, perfect justice, to say nothing of the beauty and happiness which our spirit intuits must be possible, ultimately ends in contradiction and confusion. A more penetrating metaphysical view will show, rather, that there is an Absolute reality behind this world, the full nature of which the mind cannot grasp. And thus it is apparent that the goal of life cannot be its perfection by the mind, but rather must be "the endeavour to arrive at a harmonised inner and outer perfection, and, as we find in the end, at its highest height, to culminate in the discovery of the divine Reality behind our existence and the complete and ideal Person within us and the shaping of human life in that image"

(*HC* 124). This ideal stands in contrast with the two ideals we have of civilization guided by the mind, first, the modern scientific and commercial civilization, and second, the Greek ideal of life guided by the ideals of the true, the good, and the beautiful balanced and regulated by the rational mind.

Life, then, is about working out of the principles and powers of the soul, the part of the individual identified with the Divine, and not the ideals of the mind. But then there must be some way of knowing what the soul indicates—we must have some soul-faculties that must direct the life instead of the faculty of the reason. Sri Aurobindo warns that this must not lead us back into the principle of any earlier stage, such as that of the "spiritualised typal society," or in other words the caste system, which inflexibly defines the faculties that may be developed by each social class, restricting the principle of knowledge, honor, commerce, and service to their respective social classes and declaring that society as a whole works out all the necessary faculties of the soul, even if each individual does not have the chance to do so (*HC* 126). This arrangement inevitably leads to prejudice and injustice, and violates the spiritual and subjective ideal because the individual is restricted by their caste and not free to find their own individual nature. In the subjective age, each individual soul must have the opportunity for an "integral unfolding of the Divine" within their own nature (*HC* 126).

What is this notion of "integral" that Sri Aurobindo mentions here? This is a key concept for him, so much so that it is part of the name of the spiritual practice he promulgated as his life's work, Integral Yoga. To be integral is to accept all the parts of the world and all the parts of being; the ideal of integrality stands in contrast to ideals that develop only part of the being. In the practice of Yoga, an integral approach would be one that does not merely develop the faculties and potentials of one line of Yoga, but allows for the development of all the essential faculties together. Thus, unlike other lines of yoga like hatha yoga, which develops the body and its capacity to hold spiritual energy, or bhakti yoga, which develops the capacity for emotional devotion, Integral Yoga develops the capacity for spiritual energy to do its work through every part of the being, including the mind, body, and the emotions. As part of this effort, the exercises of hatha yoga or the prayers and austerities of devotional practice may be employed, but the main emphasis is rather on allowing the Yoga-force or Shakti to work through any and every part of the being it needs to, meaning that particular techniques or practices can shift depending on when they are needed. An integral approach is thus able to include all the energies, faculties, and parts of the being, even as it does not consist of the mere sum of all partial approaches.

The idea of integrality in social evolution is not exactly the same as in Integral Yoga, as this Yoga is a practice that is generally meant for the few who are able to devote themselves to it. But from the use of the term in Yoga we can begin to understand what he means by it in a more general sense. An integral approach to human evolution in general is one that allows all the parts of the individual to get their full development, without the rigidity of ideologies or unnecessary social constraints. That is, "the Shudra cannot be rigidly confined within his Shudrahood, nor the Brahmin in his Brahminhood, but each contains within himself the potentialities and the need of perfection of his other elements of a divine manhood" (*HC* 127). Further, an integral approach would follow the principle of "the large development of the whole truth of our being in the realisation of a spontaneous and self-supported spiritual harmony" (*HC* 127).

But this still leaves the question of what faculty is to harmonize these potentialities in an integral way if not the reason. And it would seem that religion is a candidate for the force that can mediate the tensions of the various parts of the individual, since religion is the cultural institution that attempts to represent and interpret the Absolute most directly. Recall that the problem with reason is that its representations are never able to master the facts of life because the will of the Absolute is infinitely greater and more complex than anything the mind can grasp. The calculations of the statistician or technocrat, no less than the deliberations of the novelist or historian will never lay hands on the final absolute principles that drive the life force of humanity; there will inevitably be some decisive phenomenon that eludes the grasp and will require modifying whatever system is instituted to organize human life. In contrast, religion offers resources that in principle might allow humanity to deal with the unknowability of the infinite: faith which might allow fortitude in the face of the changes and deviations from mental expectations, love which might allow for greater harmony between fellow humans and enable cooperation and mercy, and a language of symbols which could in principle provide a more flexible basis for interpreting the world than the dry and rigid categories of rational thought; perhaps these and other resources of religion might be that which allows humanity to organize its outer life.

And yet there is a conflict before we even begin: religion cannot even harmonize with human reason itself. This is not strictly a phenomenon that comes from the modern scientific intellect, as some ancient Greek philosophers looked at the gods worshipped by their fellows and concluded that they were unsupported myths. The objection of the rational intellect to the claims of religion is simple and straightforward. Religion has no objective evidence for its claims, and it relies on baroque theoretical systems to reconcile issues like the existence of a benevolent God being seemingly incompatible with the presence of evil. Sri Aurobindo notes that this conflict between reason and religion leads to two characteristic responses, either the urge to discard religion altogether, or alternatively the attempt to rationalize religion and make it acceptable to its standards (*HC* 129). The former approach would be the approach of full atheism or secularism, and the latter approach could be seen in attempts at "liberalized" religions like Protestantism and Unitarian Universalism. The issue with both of these approaches is that they do not understand religion. "The deepest heart, the inmost essence of religion, apart from its outward machinery of creed, cult, ceremony and symbol, is the search for God and the finding of God... [religion] has nothing to do with the realm of reason or its normal activities; its aim, its sphere, its process is suprarational" (*HC* 131). Further, they are not able to modify it without destroying its essence. "But in its endeavour to get rid of the superstition and ignorance which have attached themselves to religious forms and symbols, intellectual reason unenlightened by spiritual knowledge tends to deny and, so far as it can, to destroy the truth and the experience which was contained in them" (*HC* 134).

Reason and religion, then, have a quarrel; phrased another way, mental reason is not the arbiter of the suprarational ideal of Truth, since there are religious truths which mental reason cannot fathom. In chapters 14 and 15, Sri Aurobindo goes on to show that the mind is not the ultimate arbiter of either of the other two transcendental values, Beauty and Good, either. In the domain of beauty, while reason is a great aid to structure, criticism, technique, and interpretation in the arts and more generally in life, it is not the ultimate source of beauty; the artists and the poets have always spoken of inspiration as the sovereign power in the creative domain. Sri Aurobindo writes, "creation comes by a suprarational influx of light and power which must work always, if it is to do its best, by vision and inspiration" (*HC* 137). His critique of the intellect in the creation, criticism, and appreciation of art in all its forms and periods is similar to the critique of the intellect in ordering life: reason may work as an effectuator of principles and techniques, but it is not the actual source or power, and there is something that comes from beyond that the reason cannot fully master with its own power. And ultimately this is because beauty is not something that is formed directly from the mind, but is an aspect of God. "To find highest beauty is to find God; to reveal, to embody, to create, as we say, highest beauty is to bring out of our souls the living image and power of God" (*HC* 145). Which is to say that reason cannot be the foremost power in the search after this ideal.

As with the creation and appreciation of beauty, so has the mind tried to determine the correct laws, systems and principles in the domain of ethics, which searches for the nature of the Good. And once again we find that while humanity's search for the Good in the domain of the mind is worthy, it is at the same time ultimately impossible—neither utility nor fairness nor pleasure nor any system of them fit together is capable of fully fixing the highest nature of the Good. This may be, in different situations, the necessity of upholding the law of society or by working against it when it is unjust. As with Beauty, the person who pursues the ethical call is guided by some intuition that comes from a source that is higher than themselves. "He obeys an inner ideal, not an outer standard; he answers to a divine law in his being, not to a social claim or a collective necessity" (*HC* 151). And ultimately it can only be possessed and fully known in a region beyond the mind. "For the ethical being like the rest is a growth and a seeking towards the absolute, the divine, which can only be attained securely in the suprarational" (*HC* 153). The ideal of the Good, too, has its source not in a mental construction but in the Absolute that is beyond mental representation; reason can serve to mediate between this ideal and the world, but cannot fully master it.

These three high ideals, the True, the Good, and the Beautiful are what classical Hellenic civilization attempted to strive for in their life, and they have come down through Western civilization as ideals that are still valued. However, they are still ideals that do not always directly impinge on life. Life is the power that Sri Aurobindo deals with in chapter 16, "The Suprarational Ultimate of Life". In practical life, the truth sought by the scientist is regarded as useless unless it has direct effect in a new factory or medicine, the beauty sought by the artist is only valued as decoration at a wedding or TV spectacle, and the good is an ideal that is taught to schoolchildren, but seems irrelevant in light of the many workaday compromises that are needed in human organizations and endeavors. The main business of life is life itself. "This is the life-power in us, the vitalistic, the dynamic nature. Its whole principle and aim is to be, to assert its existence, to increase, to expand, to possess and to enjoy: its native terms are growth of being, pleasure and power" (*HC* 156). Further, our modern Western civilization is based around the idea of the fulfillment of life-power, using it for the purposes of grand economic, political, and social organization. In contrast, in Sri Aurobindo's view, "The ancients regarded this life as an occasion for the development of the rational, the ethical, the aesthetic, the spiritual being"; he cited the focus on philosophy and poetry in Greek and Roman civilization and the high value placed on religious seeking in India (*HC* 158).

The modern outward commercial view of life operates on two levels, the individual and the collective. The individual in this societal arrangement is allowed, or even encouraged, to pursue their own self-interest in acquiring wealth, possessions, and status. Fukuyama observed that after the decline of aristocratic value systems, the ideal for the individual in modern Western society is the "bourgeois" life spent in pursuit of individual gain and success, and in modern societies this is held in fact as a valid moral ideal because it allows for the satisfaction of human desires without risking the conflict and destruction that can result from battles for primacy according to the aristocratic ideal (Fukuyama 185). But though the doctrine of individual self-interest is a major part of the modern worldview, there is a collective aspect to it as well. The tension between the individual and the collective is a longstanding problem of social and political organization in all human societies, but there is a specific aspect of it that is activated by the problem of industrial modernity. With industrial modernity, economies have become more complex than ever before, requiring specialized engineering knowledge, globally distributed supply chains and trade regimes, and allocating human capital is a major issue. Rather than being a complex but self-regulating organic being, deliberate specialized knowledge needs to be applied at the economic and political levels to address social and economic issues; hence the perception that industrial society is a giant machine in which individual humans are cogs, rather than self-interested rational agents with absolute freedom. This is the collectivism which is the result of the outward Western ideal of life, and the dueling ideologies of the 20th century, communism, fascism, and liberalism, were attempts to deal with the problems of organizing these collective machines.

This outward view of the goal and legitimating principle of society is, of course, in direct tension with Sri Aurobindo's idea that the ultimate aim of life is the expression of the Divine. "On this a great deal hangs; for if the practical and vitalistic view of life and society is the right one, if society merely or principally exists for the maintenance, comfort, vital happiness and political and economic efficiency of the species, then our idea that life is a seeking for God and for the highest self and that society too must one day make that its principle cannot stand" (HC 159). But this truly spiritual life, if it actually exists, must be able to deal with the dynamic life-power in humanity. A pursuit of only the high ideals of Truth, Good, and Beauty in their forms of philosophy, saintliness, and art would not be a spiritual life that is truly integral—accepting and harmonizing all the parts and energies of human life. Worse, it may not be possible for a society made up of only artists and philosophers to subsist either, as it would fail at economic production or self-defense or cultural transmission or any of the other tests that life poses. So any truly integral vision of a spiritual or Divine life must be able to deal with the life power that causes so many problems.

In fact, one persistent approach of the religious mind has been asceticism—the declaration that the life power and thus the human life that runs on it are inherently corrupt, tainted by lust, greed, and the drive for domination, and the only adequate spiritual solution would be to withdraw from life into the monastery, or the life of the wandering renunciate or cynical philosopher. Another approach was the ancient Indian spiritual philosophy which identified four legitimate uses of the life power, *artha*, or worldly success, *kama*, or pleasure, *dharma*, or virtue, and *moksha*, or spiritual liberation. The issue in that case was that moksha was still held to be the highest of these, and the other uses of the life power were essentially seen as meant for those who had not yet reached readiness for liberation (*HC* 164). Thus, neither of these approaches are solutions for Sri Aurobindo's ideal of an integral divine life.

In a rich and fascinating passage taking up the second half of the "The Suprarational Ultimate of Life", Sri Aurobindo puts forward a vision of spiritual evolution that is, in his view, the only way for the life-power to reach its full consummation. The raw materials that life starts out with are indeed crude and "infrarational": on the negative side there are the desire for domination, lust, selfishness, desire for food and comfort, leisure, pleasure, and gross excitement; but there are also positive materials such as "rich elements of power, beauty, nobility, good, sacrifice, worship, divinity" (*HC* 164). None of the mental systems, whether they be religious systems of virtue, ancient or modern, or the modern rational ideal, have succeeded in harmonizing all of these forces towards a Divine end. A worldview that saw no higher power than the mind would have to stop there and declare that the problem is impossible to solve—or that it could only be solved by religious quietism or a flight to another heavenly plane. But in Sri Aurobindo's view, there is a plane of suprarational forces greater than the mind. They manifest in the form of great ideals that humanity pursues—love, romantic and filial, patriotism, justice, liberty, devotion for the great religious forms and figures, and so on. Humans called by these great ideals devote their life-energies to them, producing results that affect the course of events and provide examples for others to follow. But because these ideals are not complete in themselves, there is still a large clash of forces, as in the cases of competing nations with their own individual patriotisms, competing parties with different values within a nation, or religious systems which clash; such battles play out not just once but over the centuries of humanity's development, and the battles modify and are modified by yet other forces in the process.

But the great ideals have to work themselves out within a human nature that is still imperfect and conditioned by the ego. "Because of this obscurity these powers, unable to affirm their own absolute, to take the lead or dominate, obliged to compromise with the demands of the ego, even to become themselves a form of egoism, are impotent also to bring harmony and transformation to life." (*HC* 168) We see this with every great idealism, such as the corruption and stagnation of the ideal of the hippies, or the disillusioned idealism of fans of grunge rock, or the failure of major politicians to bring about utterly transformational change. But what keeps the process of life and society moving and evolving is the constant flux of Nature which continues to propel the life force onwards with yet other ideals. "There is the pressure on human life of an Infinite which will not allow it to rest too long in any formulation, — not at least until it has delivered out of itself that which shall be its own self-exceeding and self-fulfilment" (*HC* 168). For the individual being, this continues until it crosses the dividing line that separates the ego from the fully Divine consciousness, a process that Sri Aurobindo elaborates on at length in his other works on spirituality. In working out this Divine level of consciousness, the individual finally gains the faculty that enables it to rightly organize the life force towards its complete fulfillment. The details of the last phase belongs in realm of spiritual rather than sociopolitical theory, as the highest levels of spiritual practice will not be undertaken by all members of society. But this overview is still needed as a basis for sociopolitical theory, as it shows that ultimately the same process of Nature that propels the individual towards the Divine realization also propels the life force of society. And we arrive at the same lesson, that it is not the mind which will regulate this process but the ongoing evolution of the life force moving towards suprarational ideals.

But the question still remains as to the power that is to reconcile these ideals, since as long as human consciousness remains at the mental level, the suprarational ideals must work through the human mind, and cause all the same problems of conflict because of the incomplete nature of mental representation and knowledge. While this overview gives us a big picture idea of how God and Nature work out human history, we are still left with the question of how we should decide to guide human life, either individually or collectively, from the place we find ourselves as thinking and willing beings. We come back once again to the fact that for most of human history, having religion as the guiding force of society "has always been more or less the normal state of the human mind and of human societies, or if not quite that, yet a notable and prominent part of their complex tendencies" (*HC* 173). And yet it is by a true progress of modern society informed by scientific reason that we have banished some of the regressive aspects of religion, such as its tendency towards dogma, fanaticism, and intolerance. While the presence of those aspects in some specific religions cannot completely invalidate the importance of religion altogether, there is a justified modern attitude that "historically and as a matter of fact the accredited religions and their hierarchs and exponents have too often been a force for retardation, have too often thrown their weight on the side of darkness, oppression and ignorance, and that it has needed a denial, a revolt of the oppressed human mind and heart to correct these errors and set religion right" (*HC* 175).

Sri Aurobindo argues, however, that it is not the essential nature of religion that causes the problems of religion, but rather that the problems of religion are due to the lower nature of humanity in general. If humanity has the capacity for ignorance, domination, greed, and violence, they may be brought out in systems that are not religious in nature as well; the evil committed by formally atheist totalitarian regimes in the 20th century is frequently used as an example for this point. The essence of the misunderstanding is viewing religion in terms of its external organized forms and symbols instead of its essential nature of searching for God. "It is true in a sense that religion should be the dominant thing in life, its light and law, but religion as it should be and is in its inner nature, its fundamental law of being, a seeking after God, the cult of spirituality, the opening of the deepest life of the soul to the indwelling Godhead, the eternal Omnipresence" (*HC* 177). Sri Aurobindo calls this "true religion" as opposed to the "religionism" that is caught in narrowness, rigidity, and dogma.

However, there is still a complication in allowing this "true religion" to govern life, which is that there is a tendency of an absolute spiritual seeking to turn towards God at the expense of life in the world. This has been a recurrent thought and motivation in the history of spiritual seeking, occurring in such forms as the

Hindu practice of *sanyassi* or renunciation, the Buddhist admonition to seek release from the sorrowful cycle of existence, the Gnostic vision of the material universe as the product of a malevolent demiurge, and the despair of the possibilities of worldly life found in Christianity in the Middle Ages. The outwardly dynamic life of Western society in the modern period has rejected this pessimism of life in the world—but often at the cost of denying the reality of the spirit. A mode of life which denies the spiritual dimension of human existence cannot be truly integral, that is, accounting for and harmonizing all the aspects of existence. The error made by these overzealous world-denying attempts at "true religion," is not seeing that life itself is a power of God and needs to be fulfilled and harmonized in an integral vision. If life is too often influenced by the lower drives of human beings, that indicates that it needs to be uplifted by a higher force, and not cast aside.

This leads to the conclusion that the force that can guide life is the vision of the Rishi, "one who has lived fully the life of man and found the word of the supra-intellectual, supramental, spiritual truth. He has risen above these lower limitations and can view all things from above, but also he is in sympathy with their effort and can view them from within; he has the complete inner knowledge and the higher surpassing knowledge. Therefore he can guide the world humanly as God guides it divinely, because like the Divine he is in the life of the world and yet above it" (*HC* 180). It is not the limited intellectual reason nor the irrational and dogmatic system of religionism that has the power to direct the life of society, but the spiritual vision of the one who has seen the truth of both God and life, the Rishi. And this is not a code or dog-whistle to signal support for an attempt at a theocratic mental system, as Sri Aurobindo affirms that freedom is the highest law of the soul as it follows this spiritual vision. "Spirituality respects the freedom of the human soul, because it is itself fulfilled by freedom; and the deepest meaning of freedom is the power to expand and grow towards perfection by the law of one's own nature, *dharma*" (*HC* 181). Freedom of the soul being guided by the deepest spiritual vision—this is the force that is the truly rightful guide to the unfolding life of human society.

The Unfolding of the Rational Age

We have seen that civilization's attempts to guide the life of society using the mind are doomed to failure, and it is the world-affirming spiritual vision, or "true religion", that is the proper guide for society. Mind is always a partial construction that fails to account for the entire contents of the Absolute, and thus it is always flustered, as its systems are always brought to some end. We discussed earlier in this essay that there must come a subjective age after the rational age because of this failure. But there came the question of what faculty besides the rational mind can govern society. The work of religion or spirituality, since it is aimed towards the infinite that the mind cannot contain, would seem to be the right approach. But there is the further clarification that it needs to be a true religious or spiritual seeking according to the law of the freedom of the soul rather than a dogmatic, inflexible "religionism"; further, to allow life to fulfill its purpose here on earth, this religion or spirituality must be guided by a spiritual vision that accepts life integrally and intuitively directs its movements rather than a totalistic seeking which would seek to embrace only the spirit while neglecting to develop, harmonize, and perfect life on earth.

The destination, then, seems to be clear: the rational age will inevitably end, and the subjective spiritual age will be ushered in. The only problem is that we are currently still in the rational age with no obvious way out. It's true that in recent years there has been no shortage of instances of individuals and groups falling prey to irrationalism, and there have also been discussions about epistemological questions in the sphere of public reason. However, the basis of society is still rationalistic, as the government, media, business, technology, and military are all run according to rational principles and structures; access to fundamental education is relatively widely spread across the population so that citizens are able to participate in society on a rational basis. In other words, rationality seems to permeate every aspect of life and it is not clear why or how that would change. There is also a further question: if the eventual aim of the Divine was a subjective age which did not place its highest value on the intellectual reason, why did society go through the age of the intellect at all? In chapters 18-20, Sri Aurobindo considers these questions.

Societies start out in the "infrarational" ranges that come before that rational age. (In these chapters, Sri Aurobindo collapses the symbolic, typal, and conventional stages into the category "infrarational" because they come before the rational age.) However, just because the basis of the society is not fully rational, that does not mean that the mind in these societies is fully not active; throughout his work Sri Aurobindo notes that man is a "mental being," a being possessing a mind as its characteristic faculty. In these infrarational stages, which generally operate according to custom and instinct, there is still some more or less free operation of the mind, even though it may work in ways that are not familiar to our patterns of rational discourse. Further, they may have a spiritual worldview involving a divinity, even if it is not philosophically articulated. Entire societies and civilizations can form around the infrarational principle; that is, the rational ordering of life is not required for society to function, and many ancient societies were of this type. Within such a society, it is possible for the light of spiritual awareness or knowledge to start descending into a few members of the society, which may unite into a small group. As this spiritual force or intellectual power grows, it may start to diffuse outside of that small group (*HC* 186).

However, Sri Aurobindo argues that so long as the mass of the society is at an infrarational level, a societal configuration like this is not stable. The inspirations of spiritual or intellectual knowledge moving to the masses must turn into fossilized superstitions and rituals because the infrarational mind is not able to understand them on their own terms, and their true power cannot stay; further, it may even lead to the knowledgeable group being harmed or dragged down to the lower level, for example in the case of persecution of those following the Western Esoteric Tradition in the Middle Ages. Unless the whole society is ready to be lifted to the rational level, the best that can be done is the preservation of knowledge among a small group, like a priesthood or secret society. Therefore, spirituality is not fully secure in a society until the society has reached the rational level.

Sri Aurobindo characterized the rational age of society which our Western society is currently in, as a "rapidly accelerated attempt to discover and work out the right principle and secure foundations of a rational system of society" (*HC* 192). The European Enlightenment is generally regarded as the start of this project, and the attempts to construct rational systems of government in France after the French Revolution and in America after the American Revolution have been among the most forceful assertions of the idea. In chapter 19, "The Curve of the Rational Age", Sri Aurobindo offers a sweeping overview and critique of this attempt. First, the fact that the mind is guiding society and trying to perfect it, as opposed to letting the older customs and traditions of society continue to play out, means that this period "resolved itself into a constant series of radical progressions" (*HC* 192). Further, there is a successive, predictable cycle that society goes through as the mind attempts to create a more and more perfect society. In the first stage, the thinkers of society notice a problem with the current order and debate reforms needed to fix it. After gathering sufficient support and enthusiasm for some particular reform, the reform is enacted with some inevitable degree of imperfection. Once the reform is in place, a new wave of thinkers begins to notice problems with the newly reformed societal order and the process begins again (*HC* 193). We see this play out with respect to any number of issues in society today, such as in debates over economic systems, progressive "waves" of feminist theories about how to secure women's rights, racial justice, and proper use of military force.

Based on the trend of ideas in circulation in European intellectual life at the time of World War I, Sri Aurobindo surmised that the trend of social thought would pass from an individualist period to socialism, and then to anarchism; and further, that only anarchy could provide the fullest test of the rational principle, because "till this third stage has its trial, it is Force that in the last resort really governs. Reason only gives to Force the plan of its action and a system to administer" (*HC* 194). (Note: in this section Sri Aurobindo refers to an individualist sub-stage of the individual rationalist age; the usage is clear from context as he generally calls the individualist rationalist age the rational age here.) To understand why socialism and even anarchism are logical outcomes of the Enlightenment project, we must go back to the principles underpinning the historical progression. Individualism comes about as the first phase of the rational individualist age, because the rational age follows the conventional age of social organization in which life is organized by customs and conventions that cannot be questioned, and it is only the exceptionally sovereign individual intellect who is able to break away from that. But once the rationalistic individual age sets in, the entire society has access to individualistic rationality, at least as an ideal. This leads to the problem of "public reason", a phrase that Sri Aurobindo does not use in the text, but is used in the Western philosophical tradition to refer to the problem he describes. In a society where individuals have the right to think freely, it is possible for reasonable people to come to radically different ideas about the truth of any given matter, including the most basic questions about how to structure society. The disagreement must be mediated by the principle of egalitarianism, "not because the reason of one man is as good as the reason of any other, but because otherwise we get back inevitably to the rule of a predominant class" (*HC* 196).

However, this program cannot be carried out to its absolute fulfillment because it runs into fundamental facts about human nature. For most humans, the mind is not the sovereign faculty in human nature, as they still carry the infrarational material of the animal nature which only a long process of rationalization can change. As a result, public reason generally works not towards consensus about the good but rather as a contending field of justifications that support various interests. Thus there will still be a trend towards a privileged class to rule, even if it is justified by intellectual and material success rather than battle; there will be a trend towards class warfare as the masses assert their dignity and equality; and there will be a battle for societal control, even if a somewhat orderly and rational one, as religions, ideologies, businesses, and separatists of all kinds use reason to justify their interests. Sri Aurobindo notes that "this conflict ends in the survival not of the spiritually, rationally or physically fittest, but of the most fortunate and vitally successful" (*HC* 198). The natural attempt to counter these tendencies of human nature would be to educate the population towards rationality. However, Sri Aurobindo predicted that this could have only limited success; and we see today that mass public education, for all its virtues, successes, and noble intent, has not been a panacea for any of the problems of governance.

To correct the imbalances that occur from such a state of ordered conflict, which Sri Aurobindo noted would eventually lead towards plutocracy, the thinker would come to the socialist principle that all individuals, because they have equality and dignity, must be taken care of by society (*HC* 200). The developments of the 20th century Cold War were not available to Sri Aurobindo at the time of the writing, and as it turns out the staunchly individualistic capitalist principle of the United States has retained significant acceptance and prestige when considered against the alternative of extreme authoritarian communism. However, the problems of plutocracy, inequality, and conflicting interests have come to play out much as he predicted, and without the negative example of the USSR, the concept of socialism is gaining influence among intellectuals again. The purpose of socialism, as understood by Sri Aurobindo writing in the early 20th century, is that "Socialism sets out to replace a system of organised economic battle by an organised order and peace" (*HC* 200). But this can only come about by curtailing the principle of individual liberty to a greater or lesser degree—because those with greater wealth and power at the outset would argue against it and would never willingly give up their privileges unless compelled to by society. And once the principle of curtailing liberty for the benefit of society is admitted, there is no logical limit for it. This tends to lead to a system where a small group of individuals must make decisions about what is best for society without admitting the principle of individual liberty, which played out at its extreme unsuccessfully in the USSR. This failed attempt discredited the possibility of rational socialism to an extreme degree, to the point where "communism" and even the less charged term "socialism" are still taboo in American politics. But these socialist or communist systems must also fail because these systems where the collective is deemed to be sovereign are also at odds with human nature, just in a different way than the systems emphasizing liberty. This may lead the thinker to posit that anarchism rather than socialism might be the only rational solution. But for the realist rather than the utopian, that possibility is nowhere in sight.

Because the individualistic stage of society has not yet finished playing out, it is possible that there could be further attempts at collectivism that proceed along a different principle than the USSR and thus do not face the same problems. The Chinese system could be considered as one such experiment. Sri Aurobindo notes that in other attempts at the collectivist principle, the liberal ideals of equality and liberty may not actually be necessary. "In fact the claim to equality like the thirst for liberty is individualistic in its origin, — it is not native or indispensable to the essence of the collectivist ideal" (*HC* 202). For a society with a collective basis, it could very well be that the managerial, political, or technical talents of a few individuals or a small class could provide a justification for granting them a superior, perhaps freer, status; further, it may serve that society better if there are more or less strict limits on thought and action, as in the social and informational control regimes found in China and the former USSR. There is the further possibility that the ideal of equality will end up being incompatible with the inequalities found in Nature. "But if both equality and liberty disappear from the human scene, there is left only one member of the democratic trinity, brotherhood" or fraternity (*HC* 203). But there could be no true fraternity among unfree unequals, so it is quite possible that "the democratic trinity, stripped of its godhead, would fade out of Existence" (*HC* 204).

Without the three great ideals of liberty, equality, and fraternity, an organized rationalistic collectivist state can turn into a totalitarian state—the great menace of Europe in the 20th century, and one that the world over remains wary of. Totalitarianism is a system in which the government does not see any distinction between public and private life and attempts to control the lives of its subjects in coercive ways (Fukuyama 24). The German Nazi regime and the USSR under Stalin were two of the most infamous examples of this system. Freedom of thought is impermissible under such a regime because the thinking individual would naturally question the fairness and legitimacy of such a rigid and brutal system. Instead of being based on reason, social coordination is based on a cult of personality around a dictator, flag or rigid ideology, with inflexible commands governing life. If society evolves in this direction, the rational age comes to a close—but the possibility of a subjective age is foreclosed as well. "Reason cannot do its work, act or rule if the mind of man is denied freedom to think or freedom to realise its thought by action in life. But neither can a subjective age be the outcome; for the growth of subjectivism also cannot proceed without plasticity, without movement of self-search, without room to move, expand, develop, change" (*HC* 206).

The thrust of this argument is that there are internal tensions inherent in the attempt at rational governance of society that not only tend to thwart resolution, but leave many roads open to disaster. Humanity in the rational age sees no other possibility for the perfection of life other than a rationally well-ordered society—one in which all are free, all have their needs met without the scourges of hunger and poverty, and rights are secured for all without the use of force. But the tensions between the fundamental liberal ideals cherished by the rational individual, liberty, equality, and fraternity, are too great, and the capacity of the human mind and human nature is too limited for this to be secured easily. And besides the tensions between the ideals, there is also the tension between rational organization and freedom. Freedom is one of the most essential necessities for human progress—freedom of thought, freedom of life, and freedom of the spirit. But in any ordered rationalistic system, whether individualist or collectivist, this freedom will inevitably be demanded by one part or another of human nature, tending to thwart the balance of the system. In Sri Aurobindo's judgment, "This [inhibition of freedom] is the central defect through which a socialistic State is bound to be convicted of insufficiency and condemned to pass away before the growth of a new ideal" (*HC* 212).

This might seem to point towards some form of intellectual spiritual anarchism, in which humanity has a principle of free association and cooperation without the use of force, rather using the reason to coordinate the aims of life in a collective, non-coercive system. But it seems unlikely that this could actually come about without the application of any force, and it would be liable to degenerate into another Hobbesian state of nature. As Sri Aurobindo observes, "For the logical mind in building its social idea takes no sufficient account of the infrarational element in man, the vital egoism to which the most active and effective part of his nature is bound" (*HC* 218). This "infrarational" part of the individual would likely be too difficult to handle with any form of freeform rational-istic anarchism. Sri Aurobindo raises further the pos-sibility of a spiritual anarchism rooted in a the soul-ideal of fraternity or comradeship; this soul power would have the ability to harmonize the unpredictable and turbulent life forces which cause so much trouble for the rational systems governing human society in the age of Reason (*HC* 220). But since this soul power could only be found by attaining spiritual knowledge, we are led towards the subjective spiritual age as the only possibility which can lead humanity safely out of the tensions and contradictions of the rational age to the next vista. This spiritual age is the subject of the last four chapters, 21-24.

The Spiritual Age

The essential difference between the rational in-dividualist age and the spiritual age is that the ratio-nal age sees the human individual as an essentially outward-focused being made up of a material body, a vital will, emotional nature, and a mind, with the mind as the rightful leader, whereas the spiritual age sees the individual as essentially a soul with so many outer instruments for its expression and progress. The failure of the rational age to have the correct vision of human nature leads it to a characteristic error in its attempts to govern life, namely that the systems it sets up to govern life, made of a patchwork of prin-ciples, ideas, and compromises with existing and lower forces, will always fail to account for everything that is necessary in life, and will eventually fail because they cannot manage the actual forces that are in play. "Our civilised development of life ends in an exhaustion of vitality and a refusal of Nature to lend her support any further to a continued advance upon these lines; our civilised mentality, after disturbing the balance of the human system to its own greater profit, finally discovers that it has exhausted and destroyed that which fed it and loses its power of healthy action and productiveness. It is found that civilisation has created many more problems than it can solve, has multiplied excessive needs and desires the satisfaction of which it has not sufficient vital force to sustain, has developed a jungle of claims and artificial instincts in the midst of which life loses its way and has no longer any sight of its aim" (*HC* 223).

A solution is not to be found by simply adding a spiritual element to the rational age by building a rational structure for spirituality. As we saw earlier in this essay, religious structures which are dogmatic or rigid will fail to provide a solution to the problem of the organization and right leading of life. "For nothing can be more fatal to religion than for its spiritual element to be crushed or formalised out of existence by its outward aids and forms and machinery" (*HC* 225). Only what Sri Aurobindo called "true religion," or a spiritual approach of searching for God above and the soul within, can present a solution. The soul is the part of the individual that is directly connected to God, and it has the power to harmonize all the discordant parts of the individual's nature, including the intellect which is constantly divided even against itself, the impulse of the life force, and the ethical turn. Further, it has the knowledge of the will of God and the knowledge of the law of its own being which allows each individual to manifest their own unique soul nature and harmonize with larger human aggregates. It is able to take up the reins of all human activities, whether intellectual, artistic, materially productive, or political, and bring them to their full measure of delight, purpose, and spiritual value.

But if the option of letting the soul guide life is so manifestly good, and provides the solution to the problems of the rational age, why has it not already been tried? Sri Aurobindo explains this by noting the difficulty of bringing the life force under the control of the spirit. In his view, the two main powers driving human action are the life force and the mental idea. The usual goal in civilized rational societies is to bring the life-force under the control of the mental idea. But Sri Aurobindo has noted that philosophers and intellectuals have long recognized the impotence of the mind in comparison to the life force, and proposed "a life according to Nature as the remedy for all our ills" (*HC* 232). Several Greek philosophical schools like the Stoics and Cynics advocated this idea, but Sri Aurobindo mentions the thought of his near contemporary Nietzsche, still famous for his idea that the task of man is to exceed himself by becoming the superman. Nietzsche's idea of the superman was of a being who created and imposed his own values on the world, and while it could potentially be interpreted in multiple ways, it was often associated with the idea of exceeding human nature through or with the purpose of dominating others with the will-to-power. In its formal aspects, Nietzche's idea of the superman is similar to Sri Aurobindo's path of development through the spiritual discipline of yoga, which also seeks to exceed human nature, with the difference that the self-exceeding in Sri Aurobindo's path is by bringing out the soul to become a being with a greater Divine nature and doing so with the aim of serving the Divine, rather than dominating other humans.

Since this inner spiritual nature is the greatest thing that lies latent in humanity, it must be this that allows humanity to transcend itself, rather than any lesser power like the mind or life-force. But throughout history, we have only seen the failure of humanity's efforts to transform itself and life on earth, either through the methods of higher culture in civilization, or in the spiritual and religious schools which aimed at the ideal of reaching God. This is because humanity has never been able to shift the will of the life force to a higher principle. "The main failure, the root of the whole failure indeed, is that he has not been able to shift upward what we have called the implicit will central to his life... The higher life is still only a thing superimposed on the lower, a permanent intruder upon our normal existence" (*HC* 236). The usual approach for even the most highly evolved humans is to suppress the lower nature just enough for higher principles like love, art, the intellect, and so on to have an expression, while leaving the lower nature still unchanged.

The key to this transformation is shifting the will from the will of the life force to the spiritual will—which is a thing that is hard to fully grasp or understand. For one thing, it is not the same as a mental idealism that pursues a higher aim without truly understanding the nature of the world it hopes to change. "Our idealism is always the most rightly human thing in us, but as a mental idealism it is a thing ineffective. To be effective it has to convert itself into a spiritual realism which shall lay its hands on the higher reality of the spirit and take up for it this lower reality of our sensational, vital and physical nature" (*HC* 242). It is not the mind grabbing hold of a higher inspiration and executing it in a mental way, nor is it the dogma or doctrine of any church or system. It is only by seeking for and finding the true spiritual light that lies beyond all human nature, human tendencies, and ideas that the spiritual will can be found.

In chapter 23, "Conditions for the Coming of a Spiritual Age", Sri Aurobindo discusses some of the implications that this spiritual evolution would have for society at large. First, the spiritual change would have to happen first in a small group of humans, as it is not realistic to imagine that the entirety of society would be able to do the rigorous and high-level spiritual discipline needed to effect the spiritual change. In addition to this spiritual vanguard, "there must be at the same time a mass, a society, a communal mind or at the least the constituents of a group-body, the possibility of a group-soul which is capable of receiving and effectively assimilating, ready to follow and effectively arrive" at the spiritual change by being receptive to the example set by the spiritual vanguard (*HC* 247). But the mass must still have some preliminary readiness if this is to be successful. One sign of this readiness could be the openness of the mass to subjective or spiritual ideas such as the soul and the idea of inner growth as well as a trend towards subjectivity in disciplines like psychology, philosophy, and art.

Sri Aurobindo notes that the subjective age of any given society might stop before reaching the true spiritual conception; one can imagine a rational age leading to a subjective age that is fully centered on the emotional life, or an intellectualized philosophical seeking. However, there are signs in our current society that indicate that the subjective age is indeed tipping in a spiritual direction, such as the trend of workers in subjective fields like art and psychology being drawn to spiritual principles. The most characteristic turn, however, would be one that our society has not yet made: viewing the Spirit as the foundation of reality, as opposed to viewing matter as the ultimate bedrock of reality as we do in the mainstream societal framework based on materialist science. Such a society would have as its aim "the revealing and finding of the divine Self in man" in all its activities, including "its education, its knowledge, its science, its ethics, its art, its economical and political structure" (*HC* 256). But this would need to be undertaken in a state of spiritual freedom, not under the regulation of any fixed interpretation of the Divine; in addition this must be an outward freedom that must even extend to political arrangements, as they are the outward structures that humanity lives within. Here he is critical of the sufficiency of authoritarian political structures from either the right or the left. "It [the spiritual age] will not try to make man perfect by machinery or keep him straight by tying up all his limbs. It will not present to the member of the society his higher self in the person of the policeman, the official and the corporal, nor, let us say, in the form of a socialistic bureaucracy or a Labour Soviet" (*HC* 258).

The fulfillment of the spiritual age could only come when "each man will be not a law to himself, but the law, the divine Law" (*HC* 259). Such a society would have no imposing power structure keeping order over humanity by force, and therefore would appear to be anarchist by present standards. His earlier critique of anarchism was of the rationalistic kind in which the mind still tries to rule life by mental systems and principles; he predicted that this variety would fail because of the inability of the mind to control the infrarational elements of humanity without the use of force. However, the harmonizing force of the spiritual will and power could lead to a different result if the principle of true spiritual fraternity was widespread in the society. This could only happen "when the common mind of man begins to be alive to these [spiritual] truths" (*HC* 260). Until that time, the spiritual element in society must progress forward in fits and starts, advancing a few, influencing the many if possible, but perhaps still overcome on the whole by the pull of the lower nature until the spiritual age is ready.

This is the nature of the work to be done: a taking up of the Divine force or energy, and using it to transform all the details and difficulties of the material world. Necessarily it must start with the most spiritually intrepid, but eventually the ideas must grow and influence even those who are not specifically prepared for spiritual endeavor so that there is a solid enough base for the spiritual movement. Opening to this calling to take up and transform the world was in Sri Aurobindo's view the highest good that can be done for the world. "Therefore the individuals who will most help the future of humanity in the new age will be those who will recognise a spiritual evolution as the destiny and therefore the great need of the human being" (*HC* 265).

Conclusion

While *The Human Cycle* is a work of sociopolitical thought, in the end we see that Sri Aurobindo's view of society's evolution and purpose cannot be separated from his theory of spiritual evolution in which humanity is compelled to realize higher and higher levels of the spirit. In his other major works *The Life Divine* and *The Synthesis of Yoga*, he goes into great detail about metaphysics and individual spiritual practice, respectively, within an evolutionary spiritual worldview, but does not address the societal context in which these function. In these other texts, larger human aggregates are acknowledged, in that all phenomena in the universe are manifestations of the Divine, but their dynamics are not specifically addressed. But as he argues in *The Human Cycle*, the intermediate human aggregates that humanity participates in have their own evolutionary principle. Societies move through successive ages, the symbolic, typal, conventional, individualist/rational, and subjective. Our current society remains at the individual/rational level with the potential to move into a subjective, and more specifically spiritual age. This spiritual age would allow for the fulfillment of all of humanity's potentials both individually and collectively, and would allow for an unprecedented level of intersubjective harmony. But the progression to the spiritual age is not guaranteed. Just as the evolution of humanity from lower life forms could have been derailed by any number of natural obstacles, so are there problems that could prevent the spiritual age from coming about. In particular, the rational age that we are currently working our way through has a number of potentially fatal internal contradictions, and we must be vigilant against forces that would lead to a backslide to lower levels of development.

Sri Aurobindo was able to penetrate to the heart of the contradictions of the rational age, seeing how the Enlightenment and its great ideals of liberty, equality, and fraternity carried the seeds of socialism, communism and even fascism. In part, this is due to his deep background in political and social thinking which included a period of actively working towards India's political freedom. But it was equally due to a keen knowledge of human nature acquired through life experience as well as the spiritual discipline of Yoga. Indeed, he affirmed constantly in his work that the purely intellectual thinker is apt to be misled by the rigid constructions of their thought when trying to understand the inexhaustible variation of Nature. While this text contains apt observations and forceful arguments, the intellect by itself would not be able to create the vision that is on display here; it should not be underemphasized how much spiritual intuition and vision the text contains. There is an essentially visionary image at the heart of it—that of a perception that goes beyond the rational mind and into the realm of the subjective inner being, or even into the soul, which will be able to order the life of society; it can only be fully understood by a reader who shares the same intuition, or is at least open to it. Sri Aurobindo's method is to lead the mind towards this visionary state, showing that there is a method and an underlying logic to it, and accounting for the many thought-bridges that must be built along the way. Still, all those who do not share this vision—and are thus not directly addressed by the text—will nonetheless have an important part in the scheme. For they also take part in the evolutionary process he describes, being pushed, pulled, or called by the large idea-forces that shape the world and direct it towards the Divine end—like the large countries, the still-powerful forces of heredity, and the large political ideals that shape humanity's thought.

In Sri Aurobindo's vision, these forces are so many powers of the Divine working to bring about the spiritual age; life will not stop then but will continue forward from there to the highest possible perfection that is attainable. This history does not proceed in a straight line towards a single homogeneous end state, but rather moves in a pattern closer to a spiral. Human development is not a linear progression in only one direction after we discover physical science; there are still multiple directions of the progressive path, and progress will eventually include principles which have seemingly been left behind, as well as new principles that may seem to be in contradiction to the current consensus. The forces of the Divine are too complex to be fully understood by the rational mind, as Sri Aurobindo affirmed at every juncture. Instead, spiritual intuition is the faculty that is best able to come into contact with the true nature of things and guide humanity forward. Eventually a group of people with access to spiritual guidance and spiritual will will guide the rest of humanity forward into an age where spiritual principles are dominant. Until that advance is secured, the thing to be done is for each person to find their work and role and carry it out to the best of their ability with the intention that the advancement of humanity and realization of the Divine may eventually come about.

Works Cited

In-text citations from *The Human Cycle* cited as (HC [page number])

Bolman, Lee, and Deal, Terrence. *Reframing Organizations*. 2nd ed., Jossey-Bass, 1997.

Fukuyama, Francis. *The End of History and the Last Man*. Perennial, An Imprint of HarperCollins Publishers, 1992.

Sri Aurobindo. *The Human Cycle - The Ideal of Human Unity - War and Self-Determination*. Sri Aurobindo Ashram Publication Department, 1997.

---. *Letters on Yoga*. vol. IV, Sri Aurobindo Ashram Publication Department, 2014.

For more information about the author, visit
ravijoseph.com

Made in the USA
Middletown, DE
24 September 2023